ured
Clean ar

This book belongs to

Written by Stephen Barnett
Illustrated by Rosie Brooks

Contents

Clean and tidy 3

New words 31

What did you learn? 32

About this book

The book teaches children the necessity for neatness and tidiness. Questions at the end test the child's attention, and the section on new words encourage vocabulary building.

Clean and tidy

This is my room.

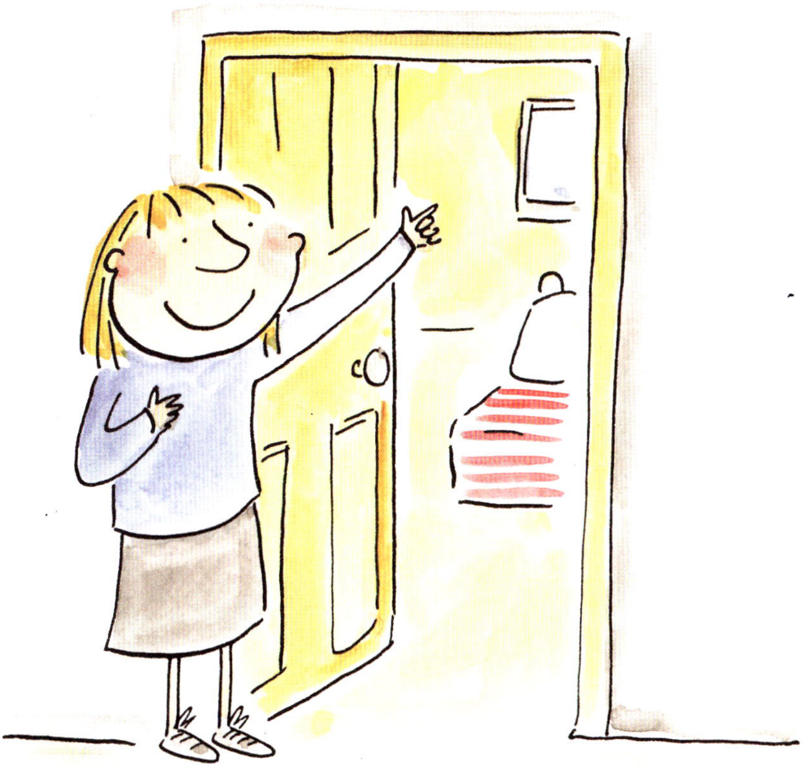

This is my bed.

7

These are my clothes.

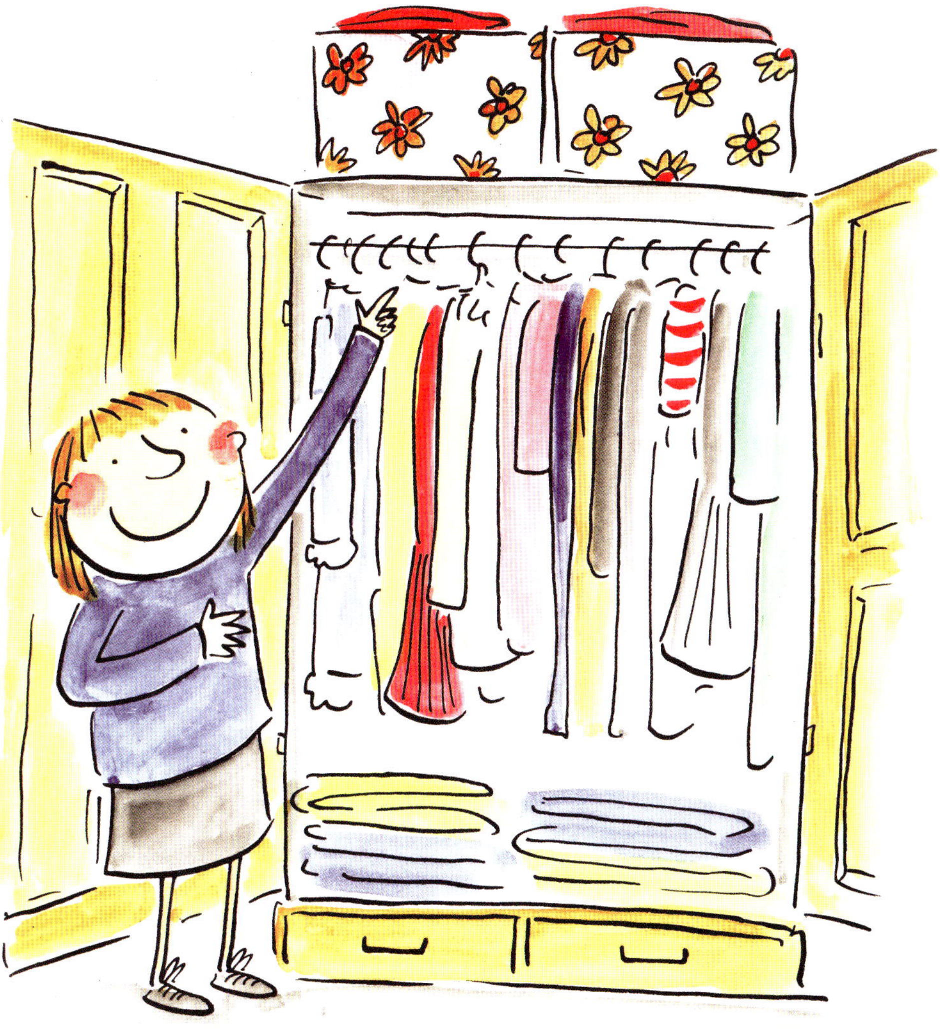

Here are my books and my toys.

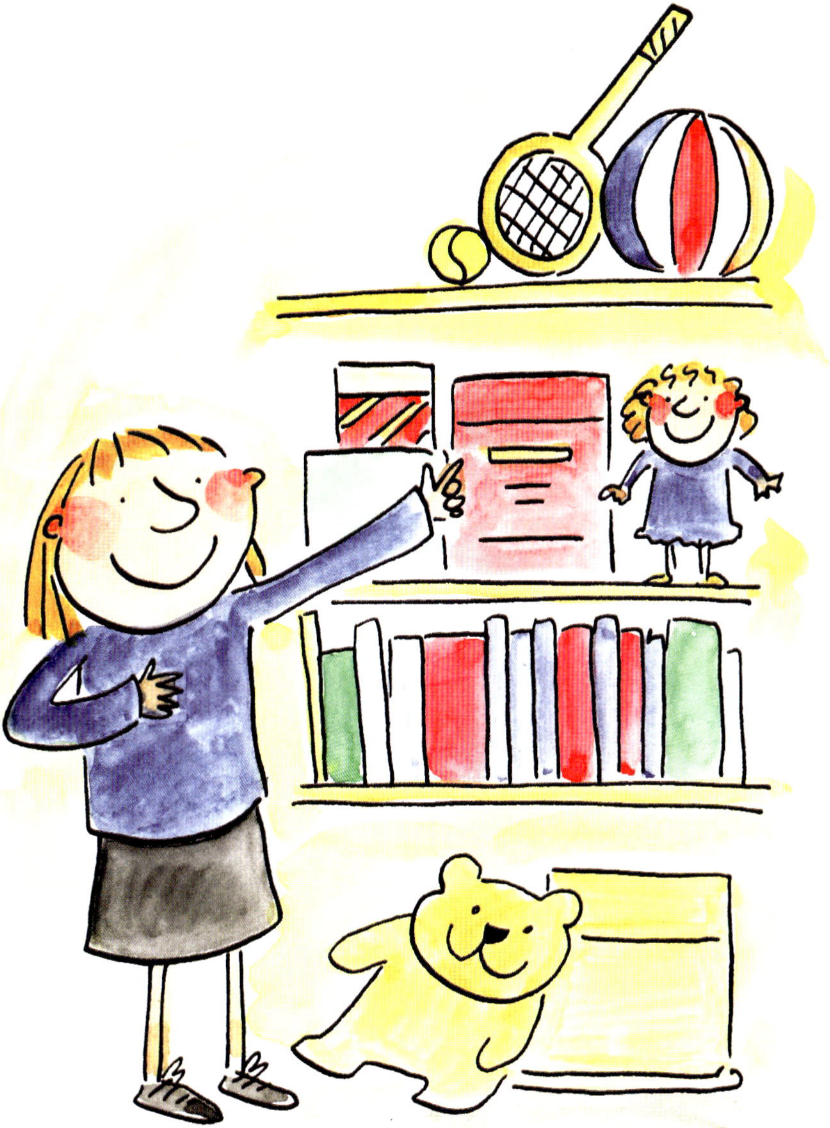

I like to keep my room tidy.

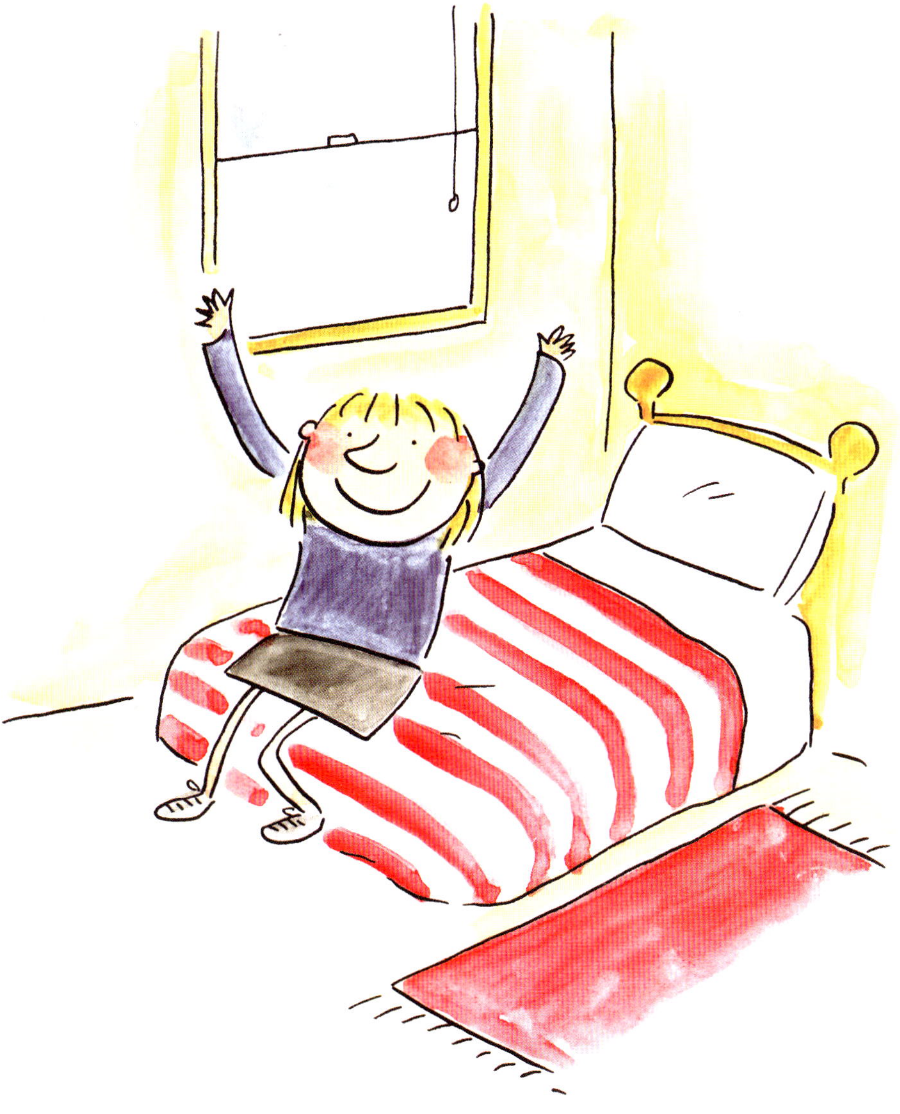

I like to keep my clothes clean.

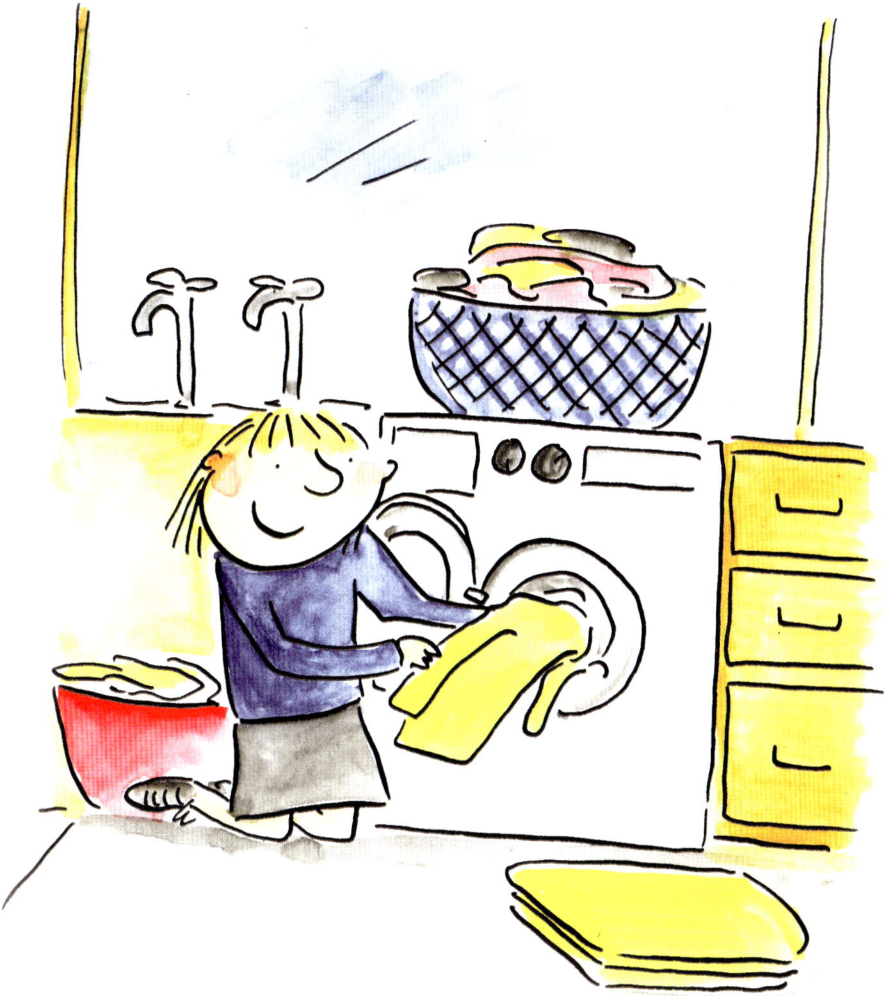

When I wake up in the morning, I wash my face.

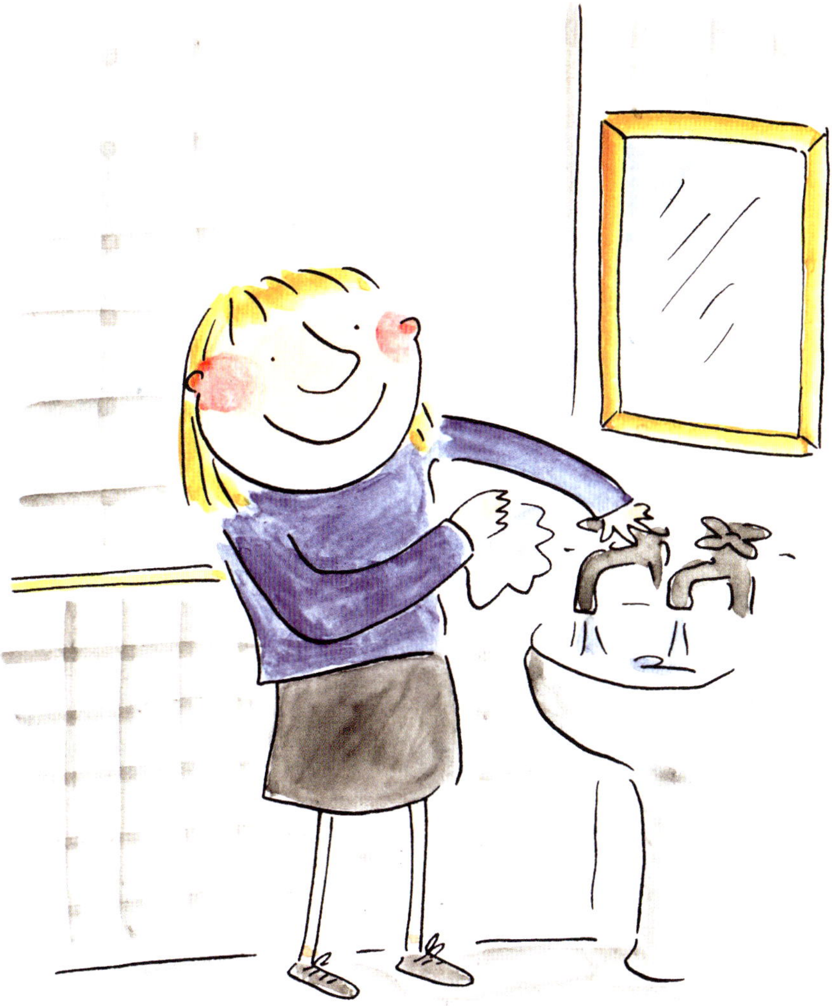

I brush my hair too.

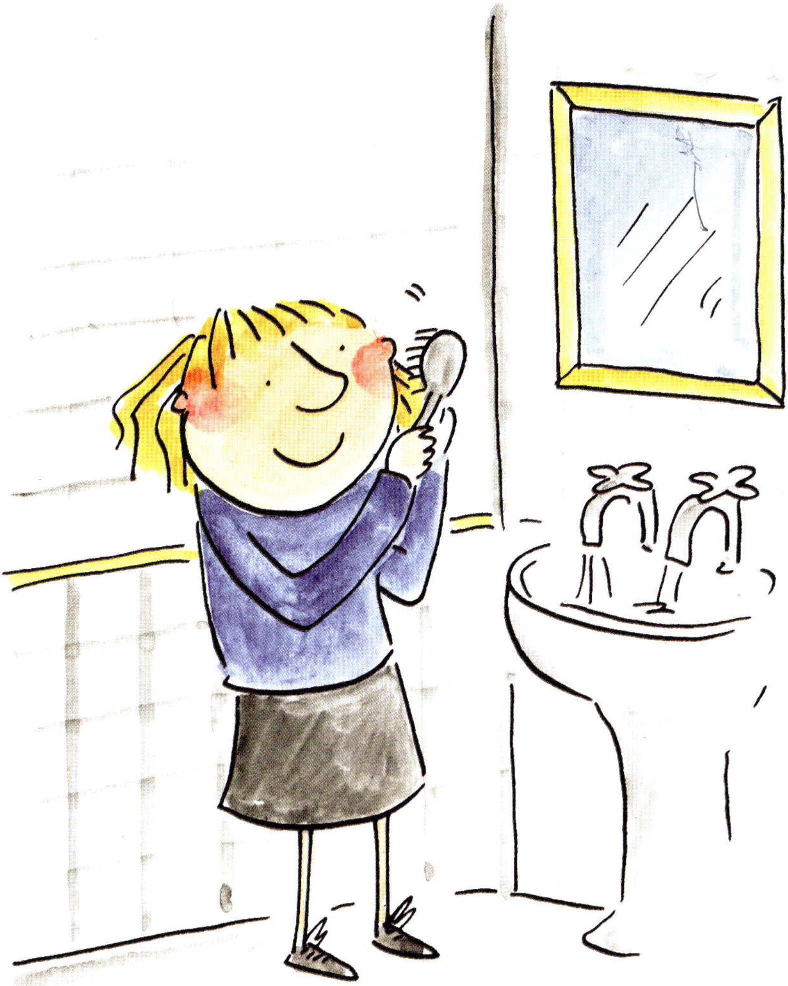

Then I fold my clothes.

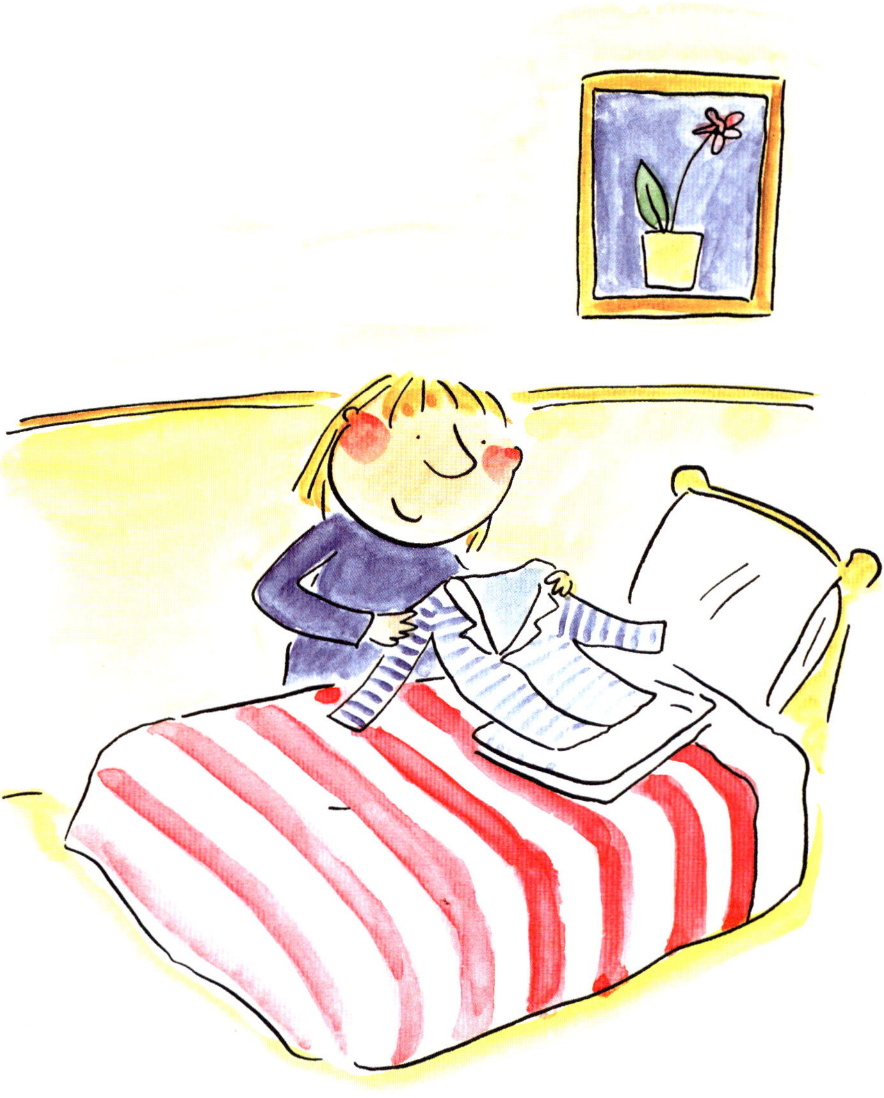

I help my mother to make my bed.

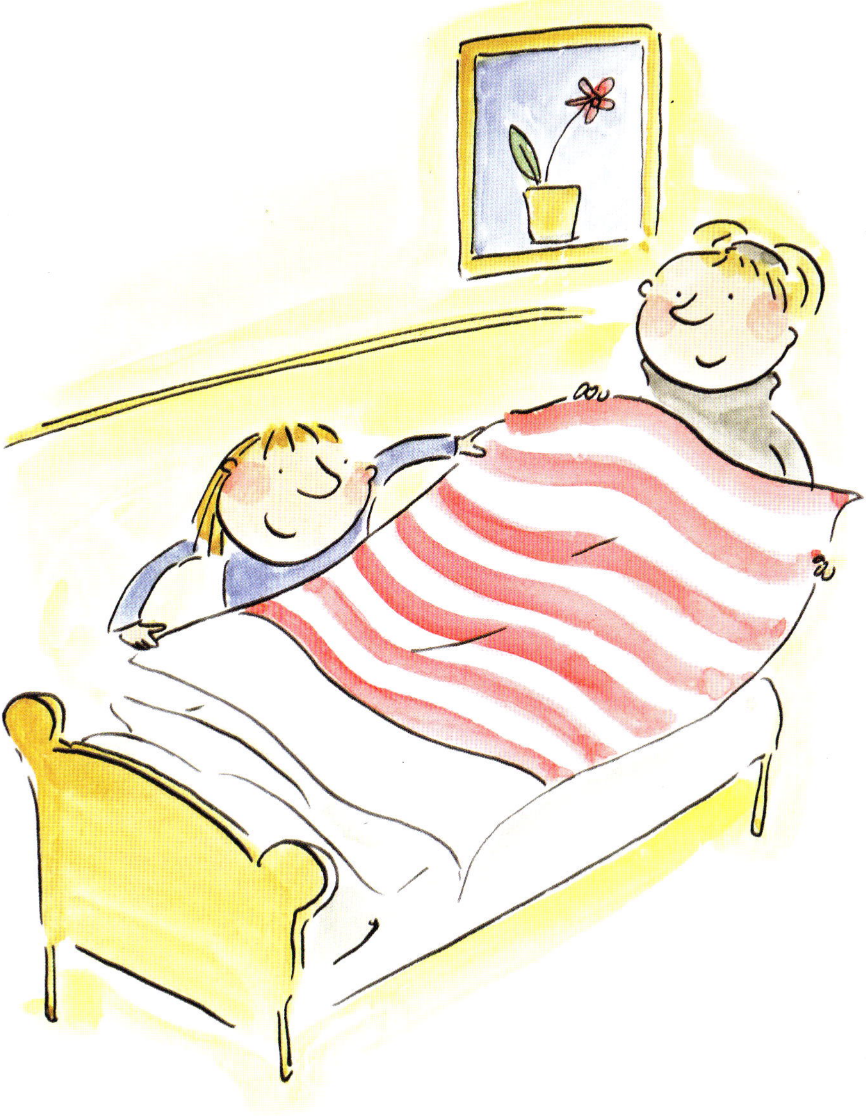

Before I eat, I wash my hands.

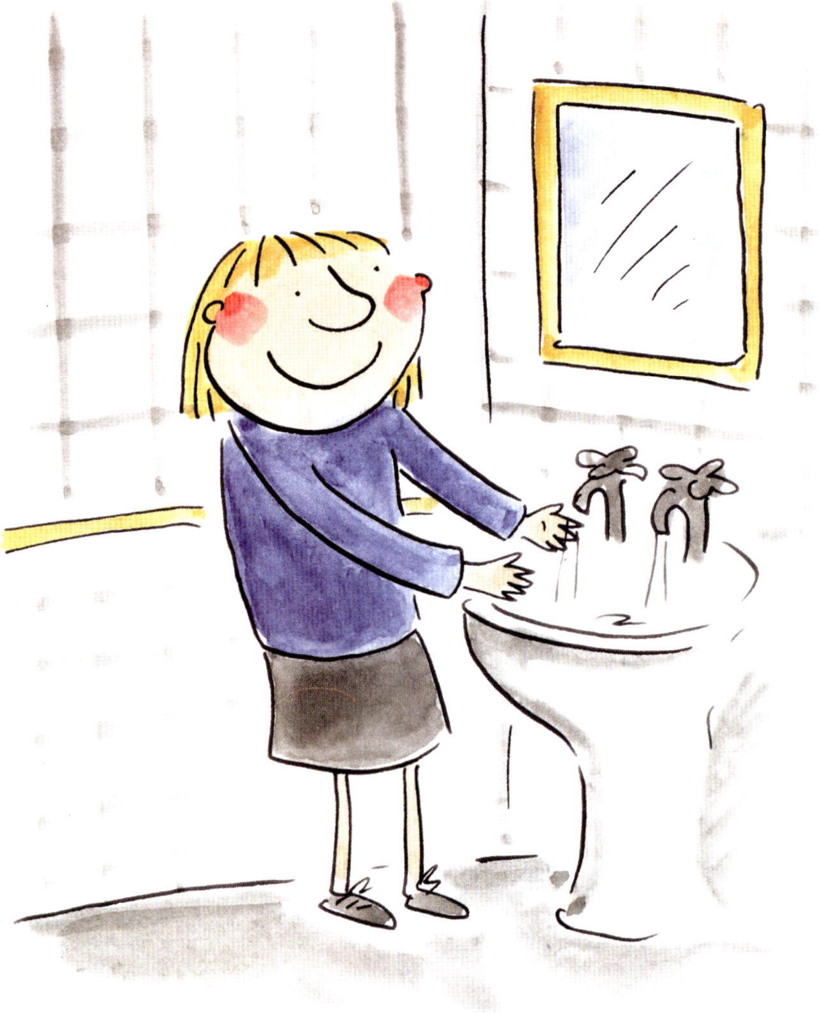

I brush my teeth after eating.

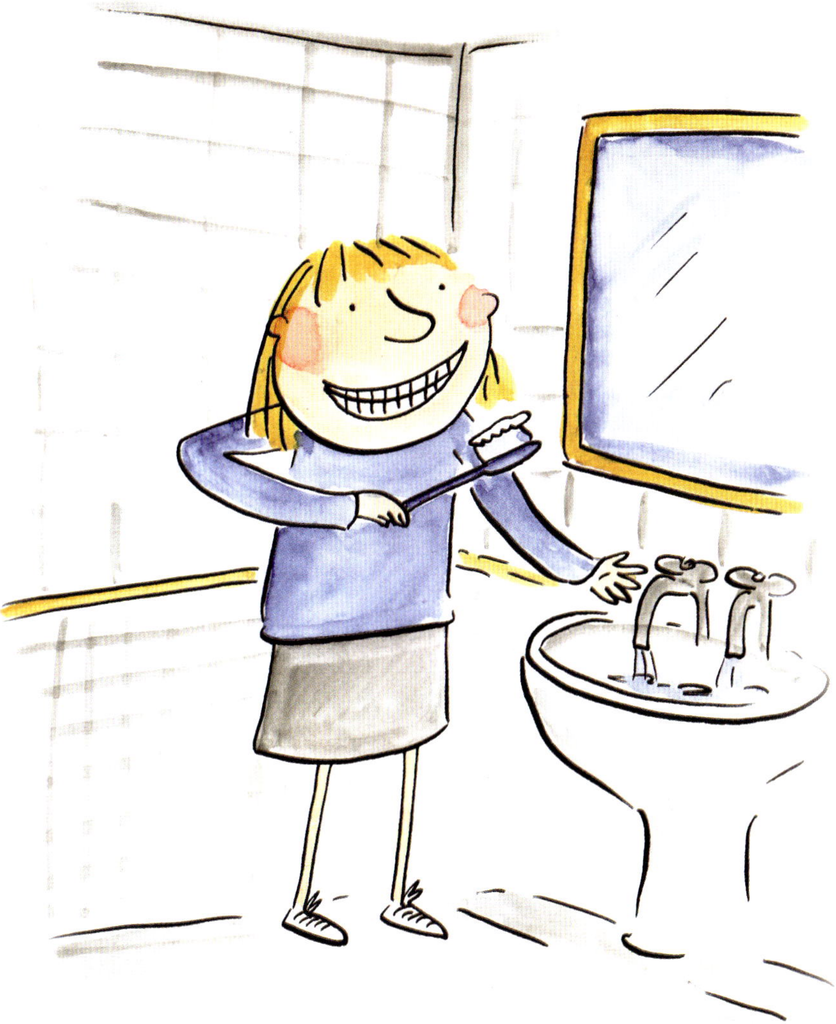

I pack my bag for school.

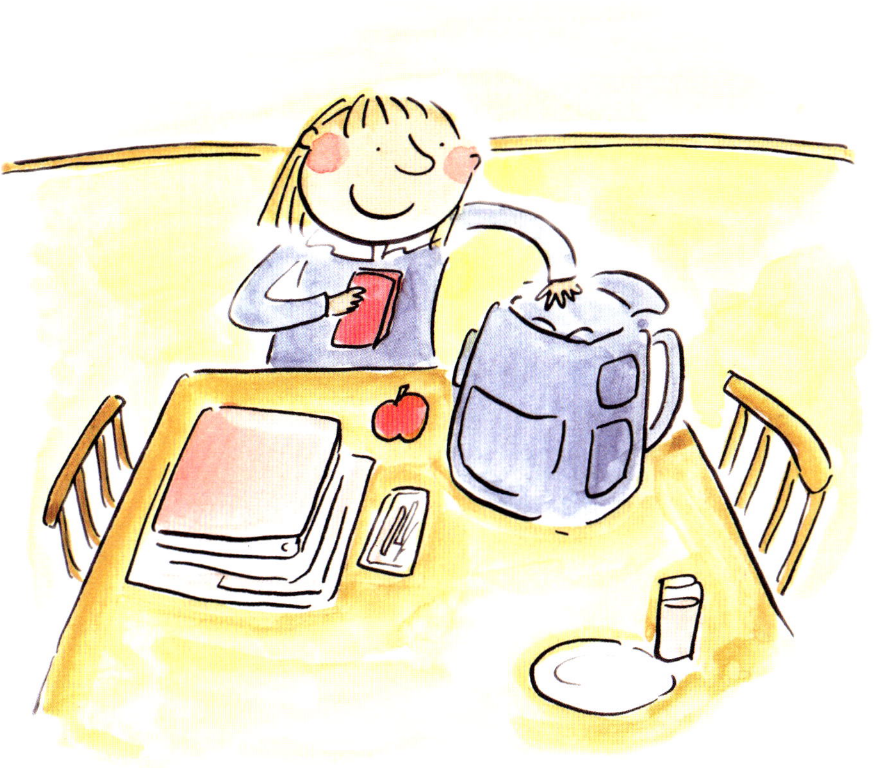

Then I go to school!

New words

bed	clothes
books	room
brush	school
clean	teeth
clothes	tidy
fold	toys
hair	wake
morning	

What did you learn?

How many books are there in the bookshelf?

What does the girl do when she wakes up?

What does she fold?

Where does she go to with her bag?